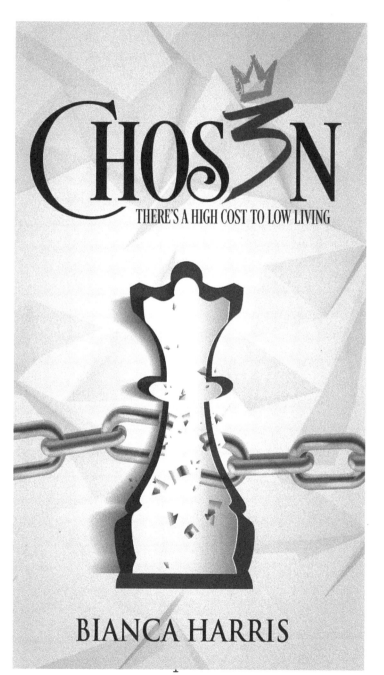

CHOS3N

THERE'S A HIGH COST TO LOW LIVING

BIANCA HARRIS

CHOS3N:

There's A High Cost to Low Living!

by Bianca Harris

Published by CHOS3N

Edited by Cyrus Webb for Conversations Media Group

Printed in the United States of America

Acknowledgements:

-Heavenly Father, Abba Father, Yahweh, I thank you for never turning your back on me! Even when I had a reprobate mind, you were there with your arms open wide! Thank you for giving me a sound mind and the wisdom to discern right from wrong. I could never repay you, but here's a small token of my appreciation!   Love Always, Your daughter, Chos3n

-Chyna & Daylon, my, my, my... Where do I began? THANK YOU! You are my strength, purpose, and motivation! I will forever be grateful for the heavenly gifts you possess. You have been my biggest influence on this growing journey. Never lay down your holy armor of God and do not abandon your spiritual gifts! You were wonderfully created just for me... I love you, my Chos3n Angels!   Love Always, Mommy

-Mom & Dad, the original #3s... Thank you for allowing me to experience life through a transparent box! There were times I shut you out as though I felt the process would make me a stronger person. Your prayers reached places that I had no control over, so for that, I'm forever grateful for your genuine love!   Sincerely, Your #3

-My King, Thank you! Thank you for patiently waiting for me to become the woman you have always prayed for! Thanks for being genuine and nonjudgmental! Thank you for allowing me just enough space to bump my head and trust you to have the perfect band aid! Thank you for carrying my baggage, because the load will be heavy at times... NOW, I am ready to make you the happiest man on earth!   Respectfully Appreciated, Your Qu33n To Be

Letter to My Readers

This journey has not been easy, but I can attest that it has been worth the process!

In my 33 years of living, I've encountered all sorts of people. As the old folks would say, "They were either a lesson or a blessing!" In both aspects, I want to say, "THANK YOU!" Your level of gratitude has either pushed or pulled me to the destiny God had written for me!

There were times the enemy tried to use some of you to destroy and discourage me, but God did just as he promised... made my enemies into a footstool! Please, don't get me wrong, there are some people that I have wronged as well... "FORGIVE ME!"

I pray the stones that were thrown from my hands will be used to elevate you to where God has called you to be! Life will not end here, so I have gone to my Father and asked Him to enlarge "OUR" territory!

Be blessed in knowing, God's not finished yet!   -

~ Bianca

Table of Contents

Chapter 1

"There's a high cost to low living!"

–A breakdown of the phrase from my perspective:

Spiritual Warfare

Living a double life

Robbing Peter to pay Paul

Addictions

Pride

Scheming

Prostitution

Clubbing, gambling, or taking trips with your bill money

Selling your soul for pennies

Affliction

Loss of freedom

Boosting/ Switching tags

Taking inner anger out on your kids due to self conflictions

God sacrificed his son = High Price, for our sins = Low living

It took me 33 years of living and a 15-month Federal Prison sentence to realize the true meaning of this statement.

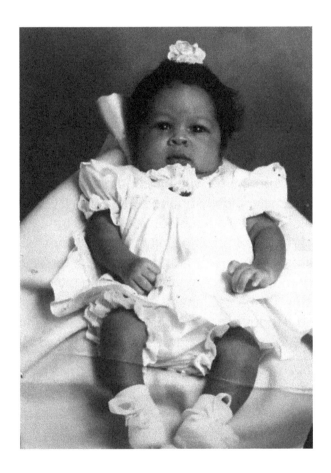

I am the baby girl of my mother's three children and the third of my father's six daughters. As a child, I was always told how beautiful, smart and wise I was. I would often hear, "That child has been here before!" I was very advanced and intelligent for my age. My maternal grandmother taught me to always express myself. Well, I think that backfired, because if it came up, it came out!

If I saw something I wanted, I had to have it! If I wanted to learn something, all it took was showing me once to catch on. I was an honor student all through school, even the few years I went to college. From birth until I was 11 years old, I was told that a man named Don was my father. I spent time with him and his family occasionally, mostly on the weekends. Even as a child, I felt a distance between us as though I was being treated differently from his other children. I remember riding on my bike through my grandmother's neighborhood with my cousins Tosha & Clarissa when the man I called "Daddy" came riding down the street in a shiny Mercedes Benz. I was always excited to see him coming! He lived in the country, but his home was a lot fancier than the one we were living in.

I jumped of my bike and ran over to the car. As I approached the passenger window, Uncle Ron, his twin brother, let down his window smiling saying, "Yunk, your daddy on the back seat!" With excitement in my heart and voice, I asked Don was he there to pick me up? He looked me square in the face and said, "Naw, Clarence told your momma he didn't want you around me any more! He's coming home from prison, he says he's your daddy, NOT ME!" I ran back to my bike, crying and pedaling as fast as I could go to get home to my grandmother's arms!

For the first time in my life, I had my hopes, dreams, and trust snatched away from me by a MAN! And not just any man, but the one person that's supposed to teach a girl about true love and the Dos & Don'ts with boys, the man I called Daddy.

Clarence was no stranger to me. Yes, I knew exactly who he was. I was told, up until that point, he was my oldest sister, Chasdity's father. Clarence was incarcerated doing a 15-year sentence in Tallahassee, FL. He only did 10 years of that sentence and came home.

My mother married him while he was in prison, so naturally, I called and respected him as my dad anyway. We would visit him on a regular basis so he was somewhat still active in our lives.

My mother is a very strong woman. She made sure we were taken care of and got our education. My late grandmother, along with my mother's two sisters, Janice & Paula, assisted in taking great care of us. Grandma Thornton, Clarence mom, played a major role in raising us as well. Growing up as a small child, there was not a man in the household other than my brother, Earl, who is only eight years older than I am. Those 5 women made sure we never knew adult's business and instilled us with great morals and values. That meant church on

Sunday morning, bible study on Wednesday night, and choir rehearsal on Saturday was a MUST! And still today, that's a routine in my household.

Chapter 2

Clarence was released from prison when I was being promoted to the 6th grade. By this time, I had started my menstruation, blossomed with huge breasts, and smiling at boys. I was Captain of the cheerleader team, crowned Little Miss Mother Goose, Miss Barr Elementary & Miss Blackburn Middle School, Class Favorite, Best Dressed, and a member of the Chess Club in Open Doors. I learned how to master Chess during visitation with my dad, Clarence.

I got my first job at the age of 14. My step sister Tori and I was hired at a toy store in Northpark Mall. My parents opened a car dealership once my dad was released from prison. That investment took care of our family for years and had great perks for Tori and me. We got our first car the summer I graduated from the eighth grade. Tori is exactly 3 weeks older than I am, but her birthday is in mid-August which beats the cut off period for grade placement so she was a grade ahead of me. Our dad paid for us to go to Driver's Ed and obtain a driver's permit. Needless to say, all hell broke loose then! I was allowed to drive to school and work during the week and sometimes on the weekend until I got my license. My driving privileges led me to think I was a bit too grown! I lost my virginity in middle school and began drinking and smoking weed in high school.

By the time I was in the ninth grade I was pregnant with my first child. My parents found out, and Clarence lost it! He demanded "Doe Poppa", this older guy that I was pregnant by, to pay for the abortion. He threatened to press charges and turn him in to the police if he didn't. His actions caused me to have no say so or control over the situation being that I was a minor! My mother and I went to this creepy building to have the procedure done. The pain felt from the procedure and the thought of killing my baby, being just a child myself, caused me to form a resentment towards my parents. All I wanted to do from that point on was prove to my dad, the same man that caused Don to turn his back on me, that he could not control my life any longer! I felt that since he was not there to raise me to be a sacred young woman, he shouldn't have the right to make life changing decisions for me.

I began to move around like the Tin Man in the Wizard of Oz: HEARTLESS! I slept with guys my age and my momma's age too! Some I would build a relationship with, others I would use for whatever they were worth and keep it moving, not caring or thinking of the consequences it may lead to. I set out to hurt every man that cross my path.

There were a few abusive relationships that made me numb to pain. I felt like I had a super power, controlling men with sex to satisfy my rage momentarily. I began to form what I "thought" was a boss reputation. I was dating all the drug dealers around and hanging with my oldest sister and her friends. Being exposed to what appeared to be "The Good Life", I quickly become bored with school. It wasn't that school itself was boring or getting an education was hard, but I was bored by the kids my age.

I felt as though I was on a higher level than they were. I was a very beautiful young lady, but a complete monster had formed on the inside of me. I became very aggressive, controlling and manipulative. I was just a beautiful bully! I would persuade my friend girls to interact with guys, even the ones I'd slept with… A complete bad influence! Guys would ask me, "B, who you got for me? You know them hoes do whatever you say!" I had the gift of gab and used it in all the wrong ways thinking that would gain brownie points or street credibility. LIES! I kept in touch with all of my friends from school and they are all have successful careers and married, most of them.

At the age of sixteen, I engaged in a group fight with my cousins at school and got expelled. Because I was such a hot head at the time, I refused to be held back so I talked my mom into letting me take the GED test. I passed with flying colors on my first attempt in all subjects. The President of Hinds Community College in Utica, MS wrote me a letter asking why would such an intelligent young lady want to throw away her education? I never replied. I received my GED and used it as a one-way ticket out of my parents' house!

Chapter 3

I was dating this guy that was a few years older than me that applied for us an apartment not far from my parents' house. He began working two jobs to please me and pay the bills. I used him and did everything in my power to run that good man off so that I could be in the streets.

I began bringing different men in and out of my home. I was working at PetSmart at the time as an Aquatics Specialist, but the rent and bills exceeded my budget. I got evicted and ruined that guy's credit, because the lease was still in his name. I didn't want to go back home so I got emancipated at the age of 18 years old. My mom signed over my minority rights to rent/own property.

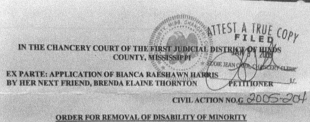

IN THE CHANCERY COURT OF THE FIRST JUDICIAL DISTRICT OF HINDS COUNTY, MISSISSIPPI

EX PARTE: APPLICATION OF BIANCA RAESHAWN HARRIS BY HER NEXT FRIEND, BRENDA ELAINE THORNTON   PETITIONER

CIVIL ACTION NO. G 2005-204

ORDER FOR REMOVAL OF DISABILITY OF MINORITY

THIS DAY this cause came o to be heard on the Petition of BIANCA RAESHAWN HARRIS, by and through her next friend and parent, BRENDA ELAINE HARRIS, for Removal of Disability of Minority, and would show unto this Honorable Court being fully advised in the premises, and finds the following:

1.

Things got real. I began trafficking drugs and selling them, right along with my body just to make ends meet.

At the age of nineteen I got pregnant with my son, Daylon Malik.

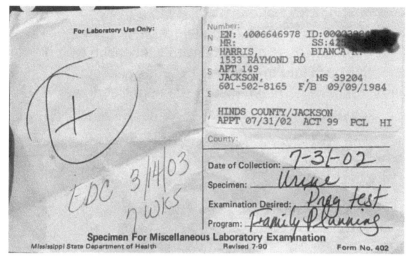

For someone who had a hatred towards men, I prayed to God every night for a little healthy boy! On the day I found out I was giving birth to a boy, my life changed instantly! I went by Don's job to reach out to him after all those years, praying we would be able to mend our relationship and take a paternity test. I wanted to know once and for all if he was my biological father.

I prayed that God would fix my life before I brought my son into this world. He declined my offer! Two strikes, YOU'RE OUT! I lost all respect for him as a man. I began doing everything possible to find out the steps to becoming the perfect mother to my little man and how to make fast money to provide for him. It was like I was having a battle between righteousness and deception. Deception won. I fell back into that hustler's mentality doing whatever to make money. Legit or illegal, as long as the outcome was income, I was with it!

Chapter 4

On March 18, 2003, I gave birth to my handsome baby boy. When I laid eyes on him, my heart melted, and tears rolled down my cheeks. For the first time in a long time, I remembered what it was like to love a male! Instantly, I knew in my mind that it was time for a change.

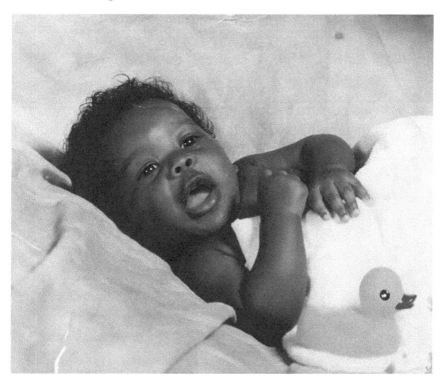

I prayed over him while breastfeeding and declared that he would be the perfect gentleman, a king!

When my guests left and the nurse took him to the nursery, I realized his father was nowhere to be found! Once again, I felt that familiar pain: Pain from abandonment from a man.

Now that beast that I casted to the pits of hell was back, this time with a stronger force. I felt the need to repay Soul for not just hurting me this time, but for my son too! "Lord, help me, I've become such an evil creature!"

I was back to living life as a female mantis, out to destroy every man that crossed my path! I found myself hustling harder than before, I had a son to provide for.

FROM: Harris, Brenda
TO: 18037043
SUBJECT: RE: Cobb County?
DATE: 02/04/2016 06:36:11 PM

Girl you thought you were James Bond sister w/o the fast cars and objects to block evilness. Shucks , I use to say now I know I saw her come out me — put when I fell asleep did the change bands.. This child is so evil I should have named her Evilnette. LOL!
Guh ! he will show you in your dreams and it will go so fast that you must keep a pen and paper close to you. Well Cookie Jr. I will talk to you later got to go and get Chyna. Love ya!!!!!!!!!!

BIANCA HARRIS on 2/4/2016 2:41:14 PM wrote:
LMAO!! Girl u need some help!! U got me laughing so hard!! I aint got my tail on no man unless GOD sends him and my wedding ring!! I was up toill 3 this morning writing my testimony.. I emailed and told Chat that as i look back over my life all i can do is say THANK U JESUS!! I was living like I was bullet proof and he had his hands on ME!!!! It's a wrap now, God has work for me!! I have done several business plans but God has called me to do ministry so i want to start an organization.. I wont give full details right now but just know, it was already written!! LOVE U, Cookie Momma LOL!!
-----Harris, Brenda on 2/4/2016 12:51 PM wrote:

>

Well we're going to stay prayerful and let everything work out so just remember God can and he will. Girl when you finally get home if a nigga even look like he's crooked with some bull don't stand there take off running and screaming help me Jesus. LOL! Then when you get those phone calls that haven't sent a dime while you were away them tell they have been put on the side line so just watch God elevate you in front of them and let them know their subscription has been cancelled. Have a good life BUSTER ! killing myself laughing.

Stay Humble & Prayerful Cookie!!!

BIANCA HARRIS on 2/1/2016 6:36:48 PM wrote
LOL!!! OK
-----Harris, Brenda on 2/1/2016 5:21 PM wrote:

>

Elbow put 35 in Chat's account. She said she was sending Cookie Lyons some money.

No matter what I went through, I never let it reflect on my parenting, because I knew Daylon was my blessing from God! I strictly breastfed him for 14 months. I read somewhere during a doctor's visit that breastfeeding would form a close bond between the child and mother. Boy was that the truth! Daylon's father and I went back and forth, in and out of a relationship, because he denied my child.

Granted, yes I slept around, but as a man when there is doubt, the righteous thing to do is take a paternity test! Sounds familiar huh? Guess this is what my mom went through. Generational curses are real!

As a mother, yes, that hurt me deeply, but that beast refused to allow me to feel the pain. I was living a double life. At home, I was the best mother ever!

When my son was out of my presence, that beast made her presence known. I was still sleeping around. I had two abortions back to back. I was destroying my body and my relationship with God while trying to please man.

In July 2004, Soul asked me to drive him to Beaumont, TX for court because he had gotten into some trouble. I agreed, but as I was packing my bags, I remember having this feeling come over me like a sense of nervousness. I never mentioned it to him, but it kept tugging at my heart the entire ride there. When we made it to the hotel, I didn't want him to touch me. We had not been on speaking terms, but he knew that if he needed me, I'd be there. He was very controlling, but in a sick way, it kind of turned me on.

He demanded that I lay on the bed and let him have his way, but I wouldn't open my legs. Tussling, he tore my clothes off. I laid there and cried and he moaned in ecstasy. Not only did I not want to sleep with him out of anger, but I had just had an abortion two weeks prior and I had begun to feel really nasty and worthless. When he rolled off me, he smiled and said, "You pregnant again. That nut felt

like a girl!" The strange thing is, I actually felt
as if I was instantly pregnant.

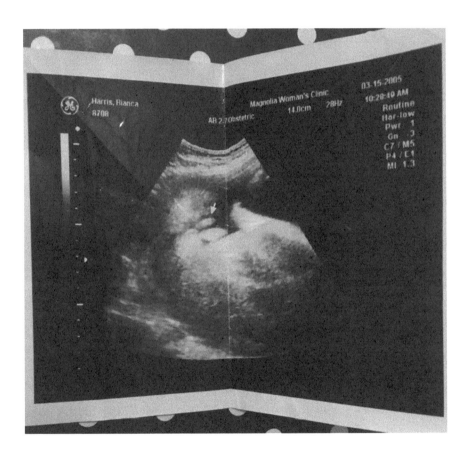

9 months later, I gave birth to my baby girl, Chyna RaQuayya. She was so beautiful!

Little Dreamers
Fall 2005
Ted Davis Portrait Plus

This time, I was not bothered by Soul's absence. It was the resentment that I formed against my daughter! I had moved on and was in a committed relationship with a childhood friend, Ricky. We got an apartment together, trying to do the family thing for once. When Chyna was just four weeks old, I began dropping her off to a lady that was the mother of someone I grew up with. She came to me when I was pregnant and asked if she could be my child's Godmother.

Every time I would drop Chyna off at her house, my baby would scream and cry for hours. I called to check on her periodically and she would brush me off saying, "Child enjoy yourself, she will be fine!" Ricky would tell me to go back and get his baby, even if it was in the middle of the night. I would brush him off saying, "She's ok. She in good hands!"

My spirit wouldn't let me rest most of those nights. Every time I closed my eyes, I had a vision of this strange man holding my baby and I could sense fear in her. I would wake up in cold sweats, heart racing, and reaching out to her Godmother to check on my baby. She wouldn't answer most of the time or when she did, Chyna would still be crying. You see, God was giving me all the right signs, but that beast had me so blind!

Whenever you get that gut feeling that won't stop tugging you, especially in the wee hours of the night, please don't ignore the signs. For three years, I let that activity go on. It was the same routine of weekend drop-offs, signs, and dreams. Yet, that beast had a strong hold on me.

Finally, God said, "ENOUGH CHILD!" I got a call from my mother saying she need me at her house right away, "Don't bring anybody with you other than Chyna!" She said there was some man at her house demanding custody of his child. I stopped what I what I was doing and drove far beyond the speed limit getting to her house.

I ran in with Chyna at my hip. There was this strange man standing in my mother's living room. The image of the man from my dreams.

I put Chyna down, her eyes were distant and her feet were glued to the floor. Even as a three year old, she sensed that something wasn't right. That feeling, that familiar feeling, came back, pounding at my heart, gripping around my neck, and smothering my nose and mouth! I snapped, screaming, "Who the f*ck are you?! How do you know my baby? What kind of games are you playing?"

Chyna began crying and holding on to my leg. My mother grabbed my baby and told me to calm down. He began to explain that he used to date the woman known as Chyna's Godmother and that they worked together. She took a leave of absence from work for a while and said she went off to have a baby. HIS BABY! He told me that she would drop my baby off to him because he refused to be with her any longer. He described gifts and toys that he had purchased, even a scar that was under her nose from hitting it on his glass table. He said that my baby had taken several baths with him and his new girlfriend.

I was thinking "LORD, you better give me strength right now!" I felt like I was about to faint. When I found my inner strength—I don't know if I grew wings or legs of a kangaroo—

but I charged at that man with blood in my eyes! My mother used all the strength she had to stop me from hitting that man. I grabbed my phone to try and locate that sick, psychotic woman! When I learned of her location, I took off on foot, because she was just a few blocks from my mother's house. The man stopped me and asked if he could take me so that we could confront her together. She was with another man at the time and asked if we could just go back to my mom house, because I was heated and cursing, causing their neighbors to come outside.

When we got there, my aunt Janice had made it. I blacked out! I don't know who wanted to kill her worse, me or my aunt Janice! After that day, I never heard from either of them, but I became very protective of my baby and never trust anyone with her again! God had to take me through this reality check to assure that I was grateful for the blessing he gave me, snatching me right out of the arms of postpartum depression. "Lord, thank you for protecting my baby!" I prayed.

Chapter 5

I began to love my baby so much, building a powerful and spiritual relationship with my second angel. God sent my children to rescue me from myself!

That was definitely an eye opener! I surrendered and asked God to help me, because I couldn't do it by myself! I began to seek God like never before.

I enrolled into nursing school at Holmes Community College and worked at University of Mississippi Medical Center, providing an honest living for my family. It appeared as though I had finally shaken that beast. The sun was shining, and the dark clouds were gone.

In April of 2010, I was going to Sam's Club at 7 a.m. to purchase food for Chyna's birthday party. An officer was following me closely getting off the highway. I was on the phone with my sister Tori and told her of his activity. As I turned into the store's parking lot, he turned on his lights and demanded that I stop the vehicle. I was baffled so I refused to get out and advised my sister to contact my mother.

He came running to the vehicle screaming, "Get out and put your hands on top of the car!" I got out slowly, asking, "What is the damn problem?" He said my car was stolen, a vehicle which I paid cash money for! He had me at the back of his patrol car while he searched my car. Several narcotic agents came swarming into the parking lot. Now, remind you, he never asked me for identification or my registration. Another officer began to join the search of my vehicle and found a large pill bottle with no label. He poured the contents into the palm of his hand, asking me what were they and who did they belong to. Of course I played dumbfounded, trying to buy myself some time while I think of a lie to get me out of this mess! He searched his little pill book and discovered that they were 90 units of Dilaudid, a controlled substance. I was arrested, my vehicle was towed, and I was pissed! I couldn't think about anything other than the disappointment of my princess. There was no way I was gonna ruin my baby's birthday! "Lord, please… You gotta get me home," I prayed. For once, I wasn't even doing anything wrong and completely forgot the pills were in my car.

After getting booked in, I lied and told the investigator that I had an addiction and stole my grandmother's cancer pills. They didn't buy it… "Tell us who's your plug?" I really began to act confused and sophisticated! Claiming to be this nice Christian, nursing student that had no idea what he meant by the term "plug!" He threatened me by saying that if I didn't tell him or agree to set someone up for them that I would be put away for a long time. See, that's a scare tactic they use for weak-minded people! Don't fall for it, jeopardizing your freedom anyway and your life for that matter! I told him to call me a lawyer and get out my face!

Now, here I was. I promised myself that I would never allow anyone to cause my kids harm or pain, and I was the first to do so! I knew there would be consequences, so I began to prepare myself mentally. About an hour later, they told me that my mother was there to post my bond and that I was free to leave. In November 2010, I was indicted and signed a plea for 1 year on house arrest and 5 years of probation. God spared me!

I was ashamed, hurt, confused, and annoyed by the choices I had made in life. I was even more disappointed knowing that this not only affected me, but had a bigger effect on my children mentally. Lord knows I want the very best for my children.

That year on house arrest was God's way of sitting me down to reflect on my choices and giving me a chance to get right with Him and myself.

Chapter 6

I was so bitter that I was walking around with my eyes wide shut!! I began utilizing this downtime by enrolling into Cosmetology school and being a more attentive mother.

I was single again. Ricky and I had split up. The kids' dad had passed away that same year from a diabetic coma. I was devastated. He and I had not shared words since I was 3 months pregnant with Chyna. My pain was more so for my children. Chyna had never met her father, and he was never much of a father to Daylon. All hope for him and I to get things right for the sake of the children were over! I didn't know how to explain that to my kids, but it was all too much for their little hearts to bear.

Oct. 7. 2014

TO: Daddy From: Chynatoris

Dear ~~Bad~~ Dad i wish i could
meet you and speend ~~the~~ time
with you call and talk to
ya bout sometime things
are difficult ~~tain~~ in life
and i know it's going to
hurt not having a dad
around but it will work
out fine with the people
in my life now and my
mom will awacs be there
for me and around me
for my whole life but
i wish to have a great
~~father~~dad to take care
of me my brother my mom
and Eden and the rest of
your kids hope the
best things in life
will come to us kids
that don't have a dad
in there life and good
will send a blessing in
our life so that we
can have better life to
live in we can undersand thanks

Pain.

I began beating myself up on the inside for not trying harder as a mother and pushing him harder as their father! I did what I thought was best. What was familiar. I sucked it up, hugged my kids tight and promised them that everything would be alright!!

I quit Cosmetology and started doing hair full-time from an area in my home that was added on. I began conversation with a guy by the name of Booker, quickly growing interest in his personality. We would discuss any and everything. We knew plenty of the same people, so the trust level developed quickly... At least that's how it appeared to be. We began to exchange business ideas. Still with that petty hustling mentality, we began to engage in a get rich quick scheme of tax fraud. As fast as the money started coming in, levels of mistrust was being exposed! We began to argue and despise each other.

In 2012, Booker was busted in a large drug ring and sentenced to serve time in federal prison. Once he went away, we lost communication and I went about my life.

Chapter 7

I had started a soul food business prior to called B's Kitchen. My hair business was going tremendously well, and my kids were great! I would have busy long days trying to run two different entities by myself. By the time I would get the kids to bed, I was too drained to even think about a man. But then, someone else was demanding my attention: God!

Like clockwork, I would be awakened in the middle of the night in cold sweats around 3 and 4 o'clock a.m. I'm not a morning person, and I can't stand to have my sleep disturbed. I would walk around checking the house and talking to God at the same time. Once I was back in bed, there would be a tugging feeling pulling at my heart. Tossing and turning, there was a whisper saying, "Grab your Bible! Spend time with me! Pray with me!"

Nothing would help me go back to sleep until I did what I was being told on that particular night. There were some nights I would have nightmares and tried to scream or get up, but I couldn't. I felt like I was being weighed down by a ton of bricks or someone with their hand over my mouth. I became disturbed by everything and everybody. I felt like giving up and running away. I was still on state probation so one morning after dropping my kids off at school, I pulled into my garage crying, screaming to the top of my lungs, breaking down piece by piece.

I cried for hours until I made myself sick. Then I heard that familiar voice saying, "Take my hand and trust me!" Although I was startled, that voice was comforting. My family was very close, but I always kept my private life separate. I didn't like to be a Debbie Downer so I handled my problems the best way I knew how.

Once I pulled myself together, I sat in the car meditating quietly. It was like a light popped on. I placed a call to my probation officer and asked if I could come speak with him. He could tell in my voice that something was wrong. I began to cry even harder when he asked me, "Is everything ok?" For once in a long time, a man, totally innocent, was concerned about my well-being. I told him that I needed to get away from Mississippi. I explained that I was tired of being a giant or pretending that I was ok for the sake of my children. I needed a change of scenery. I was afraid that I would hurt myself or somebody! He asked, "Ms. Harris, where are you gonna go?" I asked if I could have permission to travel to Georgia. I informed him that my sister Chasdity lived there and I could live with her until I found my own place. The Grace of God was with me! He had me to come by his office to sign papers and granted me a 30-day travel pass. I was ordered to keep him abreast on the progress of my transition, as I did. That was nothing but FAVOR!! Honestly, I hadn't spoken with my sister until I had the approval, but I trusted that she would welcome me with open arms.

I packed my house up in 24 hours. I left without telling anyone, just a goodbye text once I was on the highway. My mother kept my children while I got situated and stable. I went to Georgia and started working at a call center. That job didn't last long. The hours invested minus the amount of my salary was just not adding up to me at all! I figured I could take a better chance working for myself rather than build someone else's dream and struggle. I began renting a booth in the salon of a friend from my hometown. I met a lady named Keyuna while working in the shop. She and I became very close! I became annoyed with my sister and went to live with Keyuna for a little while.

Business was up and down, but I had saved up enough money to get my own place. My next priority was sending for my children. Daylon wanted to remain in Mississippi to finish fifth grade with his friends, and to be with my mom! Chyna came to live with me, and we would visit Daylon as often as possible.

Finally, my actions and decisions were being walked along a positive path. Our home was beautiful and cozy. The kids were happy, and I was in a really great place spiritually.

Once again, though, a dark cloud was forming overhead. Another storm for me to weather.

Chapter 8

I received a phone call from my probation officer one Friday morning in mid-March telling me that he needed me to be in his office the following Tuesday. I could tell in his voice that something was wrong, not to mention, it was not time for me to report for a scheduled drug screening. I agreed to be in Jackson promptly.

Tuesday, March 18, 2013—Dylan's birthday—I turned into the parking lot of MDOC Probation & Parole. I noticed that there were 2 unmarked cars in the parking lot. Ignoring that gut feeling, I walked into the building to report as usual. My probation officer immediately took me into this office, pretending to ask me a series of unimportant questions until the door swung open. In walked several federal agents. "FUCK!" I remember thinking to myself. My spirit left my body and fear crept in.

They introduced themselves and began to question me like I was auditioning for Jeopardy. There was this light skinned female agent that looked at me with a slanted smirk on her face and asked, "What kind of relationship do you and Booker have?" I was baffled and responded "Who?! I'm sorry, I don't think I know who that is!" I could tell that my stance was pissing them off.

They took turns asking me several questions from my personal life to the front door of other people's business. They even tried to break me down when they realized that I didn't have two words to offer them by mentioning the murder of Drew, my God Brother. When that didn't work either it just pissed me off. "If I'm not under arrest, I'd like to be excused now," I told them.

The officer looked me square in the face, assuring me that they would be in touch then excused me to leave. "Lord, if you get me out of this, I PROMISE I'm done with everything and everybody!" I began to pray out loud while sitting in my truck before pulling off. Doing 75 in a 35, I sped to my mother's house, making calls to a few people in my circle, informing them of the heat that was on my back. I had to get myself all the way together. My son was there waiting on me to go on a lunch date for his birthday. I took them to one of his favorite Japanese restaurants, shopping, then got the hell out of Mississippi!!

My whole ride back to Georgia was in complete silence trying to figure what miserable rat sent the Feds my way and for what?! No matter how, what, or when, when you're living that life, you are guaranteed to be touched! When I made it home, I got rid of everything that had or could have had any illegal activity attached to it! I quit hustling cold turkey! I made God so many promises that week, I know He wanted to slap me for lying! The thing of it is, I really thought I was done with that lifestyle. I made the transition to leave everything behind.

My past had finally caught up with me! I had to carry on, staying prayerful. My brother Earl reached out to me and said he thought it would be best if I put my things in storage and come back to Mississippi for a while. He even tried to find me another building and go into partnership with me opening another soul food restaurant. I ignored the idea. Three days later, my dad called saying the Lord was trying to speak through my family, giving me word that I needed to be back home. He was worried that the Feds would try to pick me up, leaving my kids to be alone.

My heart told me that everything that they were saying was exactly what God wanted me to do, but I was so stubborn and didn't leave. You see, when God send you clarity by way of other people, we sometimes question if they are delivering the right message or just giving their thoughts in God's name. Sure enough, God had to take drastic steps to make me move! I received an eviction notice saying that I had missed my court date and had 3 days to vacate my home. I called the company that I was renting from to see what was going on, because I never received a notice for court, although I knew I was late. The lady hit me with so many fees and refused to accept partial payment while I investigated what was going on.

After going back and forth with her for two hours, I got a call from an unfamiliar number. "Hello Ms. Harris! This is FBI Agent..." My body grew numb as she began to sound like Charlie Brown! My blood pressure hit the sky, and I just sat sobbing in a pool of tears. The clock was ticking so loud, I slapped it off the wall, knocking out the battery. The day had come. I was assured they would be in touch with me. She was calling to schedule a time for me to come into her office for further questioning.

Chapter 9

Being in the streets my entire life, I knew darn well what that meant: We've completed our investigation, and we have all the evidence we need to convict you unless you are willing to play ball! I PANICKED! Heart racing, I'm running around the house snatching pictures off the walls. I jumped in my truck loaded with boxes of files, laptops, and other documentation that may incriminate me and drove them to the nearest disposal landfill, trashing everything! I drove slowly back to the house as I tried to find the right words to explain to my children that our whole world was about to be turned upside due to my own actions and bad choices.

Once again, I failed to keep the hearts of my children protected. I decided to block all calls that were not saved in my contacts. I figured that if the Feds had anything to say to me, they would know how to find me. And they did just that!

The probation officer that granted me the pass to travel out of state was well aware of my location, but technically I was never supposed to be "living" in Georgia without doing a relocation through MDOC and Georgia probation office. Needless to say, they fired him! The federal agent was still trying to get in touch with me, calling my mother demanding that I return her call or come into her office. Nothing made me question my faith like the moment when I realized that they were not going to give up until they had me in custody.

"Ok Father," I prayed. "I hear you! Here I am!"

I remember sending out a group text to my mom, Chat, my aunt Janice, and Mrs. Brown, my spiritual advisor. I informed them that I was about to enter into an intimate prayer and fast with my Creator, and I would be turning off my phone in case they were trying to reach me.

I stood upstairs in the hallway by my bedroom and got naked, stretching out prostrate on the floor. I began to pray and cry out to God, petitioning for my freedom and success. I made promises and demands with every ounce of power vested in me! "Lord, if you just have mercy on me, I'll serve you wholeheartedly," I prayed.

Chapter 10

May 2013.

The school year was ending. Daylon was being promoted to the 6th grade. I was so excited, because that meant that he would be moving to Georgia with Chyna and I. Georgia schools ended before Mississippi, so on Chyna's last day of school, she and I was packed up and set out to go to Daylon's class promotion. It was a very beautiful ceremony. He received several honor awards, making me a very proud mommy in a world of turmoil. I rewarded him with a surprise pool party since he would be leaving his friends. No matter what I went through, I never allowed it to hinder me from making my kids happy.

The following Monday we were scheduled to return back to Georgia. While getting dressed, my phone began to ring, startling me, giving me the sickest feeling. It was an unfamiliar voice calling stating that he was calling from the probation office. He introduced himself as the person that handles in state/ out of state transfers and needed me to come sign my approval to transfer to Georgia. A soft voice whispered, "He's lying, but you are going to be ok... I am with you!" I put that thought in the back of my mind and agreed to come early

Tuesday morning so I can get out of Mississippi once and for all!

The next morning, I asked my cousin Clarissa to ride with me, because I had my children in the car and my instincts told me that this visit wasn't going to go well. As my pearl white Cadillac SRX turned onto the parking lot of the two story brick building, I noticed two white men walking toward my truck. Looking in my rearview mirror, I tried not to alert my kids from the back seat. Snatching on my doors from the front driver and passenger side they exclaimed: "Ms. Harris, you are under arrest! Step out with your hands up!"

My kids began crying and screaming as the agents surrounded my truck. Suddenly, a familiar face came from the rear of the vehicle... The female agent with that same stupid looking smirk on her face! "This Bitch!" I said it before I knew it! Anger and rage filled my body fast and anxiety quickly took over. I tried to remain calm, saving face for my children and turned to them saying: "No matter what happens, Mommy love y'all, and everything is going to be ok!"

I wouldn't allow them to cuff me in front of my children, but agreed to be cuffed once they took me inside the building. My pink tunic dress drug the ground, getting caught under my flip flops. As I walked into the building, hands cuffed behind my back, everything became blurry and moved in slow motion. I felt so humiliated as I walked past familiar faces of people I knew from the streets. Going through the back door, they escorted me to the U.S. Marshall's unmarked black tented Sedan.

My instincts were telling me to pray, but that beast was laughing so loud in my ear saying, "One of those hoes set you up!" At that point, I began to do instant replays trying to figure out who or why because I didn't deal with a lot of people. A 10-minute ride from the probation office to the U.S. Marshals headquarters seemed like an hour-long ride. Once we arrived at the headquarters they took me into an interrogation room setup like a board meeting. A male agent set at the head of the table with a recorder on his left side and a laptop on the right. Several chairs were gathered around this long wooden rectangular table… In walked Mrs. Smirk Face! My tension at the back of my neck thickened because I knew she was coming with the sequence of questions that I was not about to answer.

When they became frustrated with me answering questions with a question, playing dumbfounded, the guy pressed play on the laptop. A very familiar conversation began to play. I instantly recognized that it was a recording from wire taps! SMH, I felt sick. "Ms. Harris, do these conversations of you and Booker ring a bell?" I couldn't believe I was listening to myself because my mouth was so foul back then. I sounded like a piece of trash in an alley the way I was talking and cursing. I looked the agent in the eyes and said, "Don't ask me another question unless my lawyer is present!" He slammed the laptop shut and ordered the guard to escort me to booking.

Before taking me to the cell, Smirk Face assured me that she was going for the max on sentencing. This time, I displayed the same smirk and told her, "My God says otherwise!" I could have bought her for a penny! I was booked in and informed that I had to see the judge in order to determine bail. On the way to the holding cell, I asked if I could use the bathroom. As I got closer to the bathroom, I noticed a familiar face looking down at the floor with his arms folded on his knees. My mouth dropped! "This motherfucker!" I thought. It was Booker! Now it was all starting to make sense!

Me being questioned back in March, the wire taps, and Smirk Face with her series of questions. When he realized it was me, he dropped his head again. Not one word or gesture to assure me that we were in this together or that everything was going to be ok. I went into the designated cell sitting with my back against the wall with my head back and arms folded. I was pissed, angry, hurt, and confused all at the same time. As I began to drift off to sleep, I felt a gentle touch go across my folded arms. I was the only person in the cell so I ignored it and went back to sleep. "Beedy, I want you to know that I love you, and I'm with you at all times, but God is requiring more from you than what you have given!" I sat straight up! It was the voice of my grandmother!

Lord knows, I would have given anything just to have her here to pray and assure me things were going to be just fine. Her image and voice came to me vividly in that cell. I fell to my knees and began to cry out to God, praying for his protection and favor. I knew there was a camera in the cell and that I was being monitored, but I didn't care who heard or who was watching! For God said in his word, "Whoever denies me before men, I will deny you before my father!" (Matthew 10:33) I had to make things right with my Heavenly Father.

Chapter 11

Time came around for court. My charges were read off by the judge, and he set a bond with conditions. I had to remain in Mississippi until I was sentenced. The bailiff informed me that my family was downstairs waiting on me, but they had to have the court orders printed for me to sign before leaving.

After a long hot shower, I sat my kids down and explained to them that I had done some things in the past that had been brought against me. I assured them that God was in control, and we were going to be just fine! Questions and emotions rung out like flying bullets. Out of all the things I had encountered, the look in my kids' eyes and the tears on their cheeks, quickly became my wake-up call!! They motivated me to soar and conquer.

I was ordered to remain in the Southern Region of Mississippi, so I decided to make the best of it. My kids were depending on me for assurance. I started servicing clients from my mother's house, but that wasn't good enough for me. I felt like I needed more money, because I didn't know how the outcome would pan out. Don't get me wrong, my faith in God was strong, and I was still going to church faithfully--but I felt like this time around God required more actions from me!

I reached out to a very close friend of mine by the name of Pimp. He was like a big brother to me. I told him I needed a job to bring in extra money. I didn't care about the hours or the pay, I had kids to feed. Like the noble brother he was, he hired me with no questions asked, knowing that I had no knowledge of his trucking business. He trained me how to dispatch and showed me all the ropes to the business. I worked under his supervision for a few months while awaiting trial. Bills and responsibilities were increasing, meetings with the lawyer were becoming stressful, and my faith was getting weary! You see God place people on your path for various reasons. You have to decipher whether or not you are going to stick to God's plan.

IN THE UNITED STATES DISTRICT COURT
FOR THE SOUTHERN DISTRICT OF MISSISSIPPI
NORTHERN DIVISION

UNITED STATES OF AMERICA

VS.   CRIMINAL CASE NO. 3:14-cr-91-DCB-LRA

BIANCA HARRIS

BIANCA HARRIS'MOTION FOR DISCOVERY

COMES NOW, Bianca Harris (hereinafter referred to sometimes as "Defendant"),

by and through the undersigned counsel of record and requests the prosecution to disclose

and produce to the Defendant and for the Defendant's inspection the following items and

information, to-wit:

1.   Copy of the complete criminal record of the Defendant;

2.   Names and addresses of all witnesses proposed to be offered by the

prosecution at trial to include a copy of the contents of any statement—written, recorded

or otherwise preserved, including prior statements—of each such witness and the

substance of any oral statement made by any such witness;

3.   Copy of any materials the prosecution intends to introduce at trial against

the Defendant or which may be relevant to this case, including: the substance of any

relevant oral statement made by the Defendant, before or after arrest, in response to

interrogation by a person who the Defendant knew was a government agent; any physical

evidence to include photographs, video recordings, audio recordings; and, contraband;

Pimp had previously served time in federal prison himself, so he was very knowledgeable himself about the process. He became my voice of reasoning and assured me that everything was OK! My clientele began to increase, causing me to need more space than I had at my mother's house.

My mother had a catering business so shampoos in the kitchen sink was not sanitary and I had to respect that. I reached out to Amanda, the owner at one of the local salons. Renting a booth from her gave me room to expand and build my clientele. Business was flowing, and God was showing me that if I solely trusted in Him, He would provide my every need. After renting a booth for several months with a shop full of females and different personalities, I grew uncomfortable and felt the need to get my own salon suite. Upon signing the lease, I explained my situation to the owner and he agreed to let me rent month to month until a judgement was met in court. This way when the day came, it would be understood, and I would be released from the contract.

As the days got closer to sentencing, my faith became very shaky. God knew that would happen, so he placed some of the most powerful prayer-driven people in my path!

Prophet Regina sent word to my spiritual advisor and told her that when I go to court, advise me not to make eye contact with the man in the blue suit. Before walking in court, she also advised me to have someone stand on my left and to my right and a third person to anoint the bottom of my right foot and pray... "God has already worked it out!"

In April 2015, I was ordered to court where I was prepared to accept a plea. My family and friends were there for support. My mother and a church member were asked to take the stand to speak on my behalf. After a series of questions and testimonies, the judge asked me to speak before making the ruling. My knees buckled, my heart beat became extremely louder, and tears began to form. I looked him in the eyes and told him that I accept full responsibility but the person he's to sentence, is not the same person that has been described in this case. "I know that whatever you decide, it's all a part of God's plan so it is well with my soul!"

The judge had to turn his chair to face the wall and wipe his tears just before concluding his judgement. "You are hereby sentenced to 15 months in Federal Prison and 3 years supervised probation!"

One part of me wanted to scream, but there was the comfort of God's hand consoling me… "I know the plans I have for you…" As I turned to face my family, I assured them that I was pleased with the outcome, because it could have been worse, much worse! I was given the opportunity to get my kids situated and turn myself in on a later date.

There was no turning back! Time to put my big girl panties on and prepare myself mentally to enter this transformation process God had ordained for me to do! It wasn't easy, I'm not going to lie! I had my days where I just wanted to risk it all and run but the very thought of my children kept me rooted! Let me share this with you: As a mother, father or parent period, we have to do what's best for our children! I tried to find every word possible to explain to my kids and prepare them for what was about to happen, BUT GOD! I asked for gentle words and to shield their little hearts, He did just that! As I began to break down, the Holy Spirit overpowered me and surprisingly, my kids were stronger than I was!

Daily, they assured me that God had things under control and things were going to be ok!

Chapter 12

The letter came in the mail stating that I was to report to Tallahassee FCI to serve my time. I was in total shock! One reason, I thought I would be going to Marianna where my friend Donna was serving her time. Secondly it was the exact same facility I practically grew up in where we had visitation with my father when served his time years ago! I knew instantly God wanted me to be away from everybody, but in a familiar place.

He had some things he needed me to learn, and valuable lessons would be the first thing! The day before I was due to turn myself in, my family and I drove down to Florida, allowing us to spend time together in a hotel suite. We talked, laughed, played, but most importantly, we PRAYED!

Early morning, June 9th, 2015 came all too soon! We went to IHOP for breakfast and searched the internet to see what all I could bring in with me, along with the procedure for adding money to my books for commissary. The drive to the facility was nerve-wrecking, but I remained calm before the eyes of my children. Once we arrived, I hugged and kissed my kids and mother goodbye. My mother stayed in the truck with my children while my aunt Janice, Raven and Keshia walked me in. I was afraid that if I turned back to wave or blow a kiss, I would break down mentally, physically, and emotionally! My aunt Janice prayed as we walked closer to the steps of the front entrance.

"I Almost Let Go" by Kurt Carr was playing loud in my head. Here goes the beginning of my butterfly process! Once we were on the inside, I told the guard I was there to self surrender. Raven turned and ran out of the building crying, my knees weakened, and Keshia squeezed my hand tighter giving me a boost of her strength! The guard in processing asked us to wait patiently while the counselor came to escort me to booking. Twenty minutes later, a short brown skinned man came and introduced himself as Mr. Hughes. He allowed me to say my last goodbyes and then walked me to an area where there was a tall, silver, rolling, barbwire fence. My family waved and honked the horn as they turned onto the road that separated me from captivity and freedom... and most importantly, my kids!

Processing was long and drawn out as they asked a series of questions, gathered finger prints, mug shot for my ID badge, and lodging. I exchanged the navy blue dress and sandals I was wearing for their khaki worn scrubs with SHU marked on the front with a black permeate marker. The lady offered me these cheap thin cotton brown panties that I turned down because I bought new white panties just for that reason! I couldn't stomach the thought of wearing clothes, let alone underclothes someone else may have used before me! I was given a sack full of bedding, government issued toothbrush, toothpaste, soap, and deodorant. I prayed: "Lord help me, I just hit rock bottom!"

After going through medical, the nurse pointed me in the direction of a brick building to my left and said, "There is B Unit. That will be your housing unit. Just show someone this paper and they will help you find your bed" It was getting dark and storming outside. I was soaked and nervous! I tossed the worn green army looking sack across my shoulder, asked God to give me strength, and walked slowly in the rain. For the first time in my life, it was just me and Him, one on one, hand in hand!

As I entered the unit, the guard gave me directions to the first row of what seemed to be hundreds of beds. A Puerto Rican lady approached me and asked if she could see my paper to help me. "Aye, you are our new bunkie!" "Bunkie?!" I'm like, how in the world do she know my childhood nickname? "You will sleep right here in 042L, right under Julia." Julia was a Spanish lady as well, in her mid-thirties. Each cube had two twin size bunk beds that slept horribly and four small lockers, stacked by 2's. I sat on the side of the bed to put away my belongings, then it hit me. This is really happening! I was shown how to properly dress and tuck the bed to meet the FCI guidelines, where and when to got to laundry, "Chow Hall" (cafeteria), and the extracurricular activities the facility offered. Out of everything that I was told, nothing interested me more than "THE CHAPEL". I was not sure if it was going to be what I was used to in a traditional church, but I was going to make the best of it!

The sun had set, and I was getting sleepy, but I wanted to shower and get out of those wet clothes I had on. "Here," a lady said to me, "take these items. It's not much, but I'm sure it's better than that chalk-tasting toothpaste they gave you to start off with!"

I'll never forget the kind words of this lady named Charla that slept across the aisle from me. She gave me several hygiene items and Suave lotion. The kind gesture really warmed my heart. She was a white lady, but we were all the same color during this transformation... Khaki! In the eyes of FBOP, we were just an eight-digit number!

I placed the items in the locker, and as I turned around to take a seat, this 6ft tall, really dark lady with braids going straight to the back stopped and gave me this really weird smile. "Hey! What's your name?" I gave her the side eye with a stern face. "LORD JESUS!"

All I could think was this manly looking woman is about to rape me! I told her my name and she introduced herself. She offered me to come by her cube to get some grey sweats and shirt to use until I made commissary the next morning.

As bad as I wanted to get out of those wet scrubs, I was too afraid to take those clothes, thinking she would want something personal in return. After time had passed and I had not gone by her cube to get the items, she sent this sweet older looking white lady with badly worn teeth down to my cube. She handed me the items and introduced herself as D's girlfriend.

"Yes Lord!" I had never thanked God for such a thing, but you don't know how happy I was to hear that! D turned out to be a very cool person and very knowledgeable on a business perspective. She was known as one of the hair stylist on the compound.

After getting settled and going through a course of orientation classes, I made sure I found my way to the chapel, because I knew that my Father would meet me there! There was a Spanish lady by the name of Flav that slept across the aisle in the cube with Charla. She invited me to go to the chapel with her and gave me her study Bible until I got my own. It was the best gift I had received in years, the key to my expected end! There was three chaplains assigned to the program at the time, but the one I connected with was Dr. Tyree Anderson.

He was a very spiritual yet educated and compassionate man. Dr. Anderson was the head chaplain during the time I was there. The programs and study guides he provided for the women at FCI Tallahassee was a guarantee life-changing experience if you engaged wholeheartedly. I enrolled in every class possible, attended Sunday service, Bible Study, and revival.

I'm a firm believer that no matter what the circumstance is or where you are physically located, if you feed your mind with positive energy, you will have a positive outcome! I was surrounded by people from all different walks of life which made it easy to be distracted!

Flav was older but appeared to be very young. She was spiritual, even with her flaws, you could tell her love for the Lord was genuine.

She would give me a friendly reminder that I should constantly seek God's purpose whenever I became distracted. "Thanks Flav, I needed that!"

I spent most of my days out back on the rec yard near the track, reading and meditating.

Being that my dad had been there before and now me, I was convinced that there was something God needed him to grasp or experience that didn't happen and now he would use me.

Chapter 13

Prison was nothing like I thought it would be, but certainly, it's nowhere I suggest you visit! I was assigned to work in the kitchen to begin with, where I became a cook.

As experienced as I was, cooking for over a thousand inmates was not an easy task! My body began to ache and my feet could not bare standing in those ugly, horrible black work boots! Besides, I was already incarcerated. I didn't feel the need to be doing hard labor as well. I met a lady by the name of Candace.

She was older than me and appeared to be very genuine. Candace was on upper rec work detail and asked her boss if I could transfer to that department. He was a very noble man. He was stern with rules and guidelines, but he was compassionate for people and never treated us any less than a human being. He gave me the job. Candace and I would do our work detail then spend countless hours talking and sharing family history as well as business ventures.

We were housed in the same unit so we became very close. Surprisingly, I took a liking to her and she became my big sister. Candace was on a 12-year sentence and had been there for a while. We looked out for each other. We would even argue from time to time, but most importantly, we prayed together!

Every woman in that institution and every institution around the world has had their share of out of body experiences. You must seek a higher power wholeheartedly for the greater good of your sanity! Candace and I had other associates, but our bond was unbreakable. Our religious views were slightly different, but God was at the center of it all. I remember doing a water fast with the congregation of Christian beliefs and it seemed like all hell was breaking loose for everybody around us. Candace and I, along with two other women in the facility decided that we would come together for a more extensive prayer. Standing in proxy for everybody! We set a designated location on the rec yard behind D unit and a specific time to meet. We gathered four stones, four pieces of paper, and water which we prayed over. When the time had come, we gathered around to pray, and I opened up with scripture.

The sun had set and it was dark outside. The porch lights and field lights lit up. There was a stillness in the atmosphere, yet the wind seemed very high around us. Although we were sitting Indian style, it felt as though we were on a Mary-go-round! As I began to pray, I anointed everybody head with oil as Kim washed our right foot with water. There were tears streaming and wind blowing. I know God's presence is real! We attached the paper with our written prayers to each stone and threw them down an open drain as Candace said a Hebrew prayer. I had not eaten because of the fast, but Lord knows, I was full at the end of that prayer session. Needless to say, shortly after, God began to open doors and move in a mighty way! The enemy can't stand when you are not in his court, so of course he tried everything possible to break us down. I received mails saying that my son kidney was failing, my daughter was feeling suicidal, and my entire family was going through.

TRULINCS 18037043 - HARRIS, BIANCA - Unit: TAL-B-S

FROM: Harris, Brenda
TO: 18037043
SUBJECT: RE: Favor!!
DATE: 10/14/2015 03:51:13 PM

Well his test came back negative today but over the year Dayton's blood pressure has been 135 over 70 within the past year which is a concern because it should be at 120 over 70. He will do a biopsy in January to look at his kidneys to see what they are doing. He has to put his urine starting tomorrow until Monday morning then we have to go Monday morning back to them and the lab. He want him to drink more water but he did say his kidneys were soft that's good.

Stay Prayerful & Focused

BIANCA HARRIS on 10/14/2015 11:08:28 AM wrote
I know God has put his hands On my son... So, I'll call yall this evening to see how it went and the game.. The pastor and I prayed together yesterday and I KNOW God has already declared perfect health over my baby!!! Love you momma and thank for seeing about my kids! Also, we have to start eating more healthier... Take him off those white foods and replace it with wheat and whole grain.. NO beverage but water till I come home!!

"Lord, you have to shift the atmosphere right now!" I began praying harder, longer, and with driven purpose!" Often times, I've heard people say, "I don't know how to pray!" It's not a right or wrong way when you speaking from your heart. Just be sincere and straightforward with God. He already knows, but a simple petition from you will move mountains.

When God wants your attention, trust me, he knows just how to get it! It seemed like every time I called home or emailed, something else would go wrong and my family's faith had gotten weak. This was another one of those times I wished my grandmother was alive to join me in prayer. God made sure I was spiritually connected with her and would send her by to visit in a dream. God knows just the amount of pressure we can handle so we are equipped with all the right gifts to overpower our obstacles!

Time was passing, but not as fast as I wanted it to. I got a message from the counselor telling me to report to the chapel. That was strange. I knew there was no special service scheduled that day, nor did I have a class at that time. I got dressed in my khakis, the required attire to enter the chapel, and slightly trotted up the compound. As I walked up the stairs, I knew something was wrong, my gut told me so! "Have a seat, I need to share something with you." Chaplin explained as I took a seat. "You have to place a call to your oldest sister. It's your father..." Every word from that point was muted! My stomach tightened, my heart was racing, and the tension on the back of my neck thickened! I slowly picked up the phone, as I dialed Chat's number, tears began to stain my clothes. "Chat, what's wrong? Please tell me Daddy is ok?!" My father was in ICU and they couldn't get his blood pressure to go down. I was told he had poison to the liver from red meat and that he may not survive. The worst news you can get while you are in prison!

I ran all the way back to B Unit, knowing running on the compound was a violation, but I was emotionless! I made it to my cube and fell down on my knees, crying out to God! I was even more hurt because I had not spoken to my father since I had been there.

I tried calling him for his birthday and Father's Day, but wasn't able to reach him. I wrote him off in a sense because I felt like him of all people should have been very sensitive to my situation because he had been in this predicament before. Ms. Kamuvaka, one of the elder ladies serving time there, got wind of what had happened and came by my cube later that night. She brought me a book that had all sorts of prayers in it and how to pray against your circumstance. When she handed me the book, she turned to a folded page that was designed to cast down the spirit of death.

DEATH MUST DIE
1 Cor. 15

• *For those who desire to hold on to the promise, 'I shall not die but live to declare the works of God'.*

Do you know that the unfathomable power of the risen Christ has shattered the power of death which is known to be the last enemy of man? This power is also at your disposal to wield against the spirit of death haunting your life.

Hebrews 5:7: *"Who in the days of His flesh when He had offered up prayers and supplications with strong crying and tears unto Him that was able to save him from death, and was heard in that He feared."*

Death was defeated the day Jesus rose from the dead. The resurrection morning marked the defeat of death. As believers we are not to fear death (1 Corin. 15:54-56). God wields power over death.

The Scripture says, "I shall not die but live and declare the works of God" (Psalm 118:17). If you are being pursued of the spirit of death and hell and you desire to live long, these prayer points are for you.

God has promised that He will satisfy us with long life (Ps 91:16). This means when you are satisfied and fulfilled in life then you can go. As long as you are not satisfied, and you have not fulfilled your destiny, death has no business with you.

Rebuke the spirit of death, using these prayer points and you will fulfil the number of your days.

● CONFESSION

Ps. 118:17: *"I shall not die, but live, and declare the works of the LORD."*

● PRAISE WORSHIP

1. I withdraw anything representing me from every evil altar, in the name of Jesus.

"Go to your quiet place and say this prayer for your father! When he comes out of that coma, have him to drink water at room temperature before getting into the shower and eat some raw potatoes for 3 days." I gave her a look as though she had just slapped me, but the Holy Spirit told me to be obedient! I went to my favorite place on the rec yard, praying and crying out to God.

Two days later, I woke up extremely early and called home. My mom didn't answer but the Holy Spirit led me to call my father's phone. As I dialed the number, I began to shake... Someone answered and the recording began to play. "You have a collect call from a federal correctional institution..." I could hear my dad saying, "This my daughter, I need to talk to her!"

All I could do was cry tears of joy. God was still in control! Before this incident, I was so bitter and upset with not just my dad, but a lot of my family members! As close as we were, none of them came to visit or brought my children to visit. God had to assure me that if he had made this process too comfortable for me, I wouldn't have sought after Him or the lesson he had to teach me!

The greater lesson of this was to STOP EXPECTING! If you don't give a person the leeway to disappoint you, there's no room for letdowns!

Chapter 14

As months rolled by, my faith was getting stronger and God had his hands on my children. I stayed busy, using my time to read, organize business plans, study laws and guidelines, and getting very intimate with God! I knew I had changed! I felt the change in my heart, my appearance, and my actions were more humble.

I remember studying about the Israelites, and what they experienced while in captivity. And let's be clear, captivity is not only imprisonment, but that caged in DARK period of your life. God made several promises to the Israelites, but He also required them to make some promises to Him as well. My situation wasn't much different. For every promise I made God, he assured me of his plans for me as well! The greatest of those promises was to never let me feel like an inmate! I prayed the he would wrap His hands around my heart and open my third eye, allowing me to see everyone for who they were.

In the midst of doing so, He covered my mind so that I wouldn't be conformed to the mentality of a convict! Every morning, I would pray that He used me in some sort of way. Not knowing how He would need to utilize me, there were several experiences that almost broke me down.

One evening, I was on my way to the library and seen a group of women surrounding my Bunkie. She was crying very loud and could hardly stand up to walk. I ran over to see if she was ok. "It's her daughter," one of the women told me. "She was killed in an accident!" I began to pray silently and hold her, but I felt so empty not knowing how or what to say to her. All I knew to do was PRAY! My Bunkie wasn't very religious, but this was her only child, and I know God was going to keep her close to His heart.

As we got closer to the unit, I began to talk to God, "Lord, this is hard! Please speak through me, giving me the right words to comfort her!" What do you say to a woman in a place such as a prison, surrounded by people you barely even know, and most of all that barely knows God? We got her seated on her bunk, and I kneeled down by her feet for prayer. Several other women gathered around our cube, standing in the gap on her behalf. I prayed so loud, weeping and sobbing! I had never experienced such pain, but as a mother, I understood. The bureau has rules set in place that prohibits touching, crossing boundaries, cube visiting, or any of the things we did on this particular day. In this instance, though, we didn't care! Every one of us were compassionate when things like that happened.

I spent countless nights praying and crying with her. I would even climb in her bed and rock my feet while reading my Bible while she would weep in her sleep. I can't stomach losing either of my kids, being miles away from home and denied the opportunity to say your last goodbyes. My Bunkie put in a transfer to be shipped to another facility closer to home so her grandkids could visit. I had a few more months left, and I started getting antsy. I was denied halfway house because of prior fines that could not be lifted due to a bench warrant in Cobb County. I didn't worry, I just gave it all to God!

Chapter 15

On June 9th, 2016, the year to the date that I surrendered to FCI Tallahassee, I had the weirdest dream. Lying on my back, headphones in my ear, gospel music loud, in my normal meditation position, I drifted off to sleep. I dreamed that I walked into a small storefront. There was an aura of peace about the place. A square burgundy rug was centered by a rectangle bench, an accent chair, and a small end table. All of the items had price tags and were for sale. To the left of the bench was a dull silver Buddha that snatched my attention. I was led into this place out of fear, trying to hide from a strange man that was chasing me. The dream was really weird and had me feeling uneasy for hours after I woke up. I pondered on it the next morning as I took a shower, trying to make sense of the entire vision.

June 10th I felt very uneasy, anxious, and drained from this whole prison experience. I was ready to get home to my babies!! I think the shorter the time got, the shorter my patience and nerves got as well! While standing in the kitchen area of the housing unit making a cake for one of my favorite Spanish elder's birthday, a lady walked in wanting to use the microwave. Her attitude was really nasty as she made remarks about not wanting to wait in line like everyone else had done. She exchanged words with another lady, but referenced a comment towards me pertaining the wait process in line. I BLACKED OUT!!

Immediately, I rammed her head into the wall! "Lord, have mercy!" That evil spirit, the one that I thought I had done a good job burying, resurfaced with no remorse or understanding. We fought, knocking over tables, food and microwaves! Because of B.O.P. policy, someone wrote a secret cop-out (the easy way of telling on someone in prison) and we were called to the lieutenant's office. I called home to tell my mother that she may not hearing from me for a while but let my kids know that I was ok, and I would be in contact.

They took statements from witnesses and ordered us to remain in the S.H.U. (Special Housing Unit) while they conducted an investigation. June 11th I walked into the small 10 x 10 empty cell. There it was, greeting me at the door, that same peaceful aura from my dream! I turned around to the small square slot in the steel door, slightly squatted, and slid my hands through so the guard could remove the cuffs off my wrist. I walked over to the rusty iron bunk beds and took a seat on the bottom bunk. Sitting slumped over, hands buried between my knees, I began to feel bad about my actions.

 I slowly looked to my left and momentarily became frightened! There was a weird looking silver toilet that resembled the Buddha in my dream. Honestly, it frightened me at first, but then I laughed asked God to show me the things I needed to see! I asked for a pen and paper so I could make use of my time and keep a record of the things God was about to reveal to me.

The very first thing I made was a calendar so that I could keep up with my date to departure!

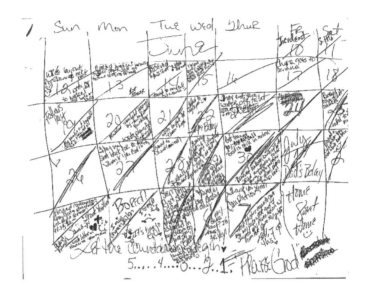

I strongly encourage you to pay attention to your dreams, especially the ones that you never forget. There's a message from God awaiting you! The Holy Spirit kept nudging me to meditate. On Sunday morning, June 12th, I was laying on my back, letting my thoughts rumble. I noticed an eliminated piece of paper stuck to the bottom of the wall by the desk area of the cell. I got up to see what it was. "Lord God!" it was a guide on yoga. The flyer was titled, "The 11 Poses For Beginners and the Physical Benefit of Each Pose." I dropped the poster back onto the floor and turned to God, "Lord give me answers PLEASE!" It took me going to the S.H.U to realize the meaning of my dream from the 9th, but the revelations while I was in there were life-changing!

A young lady was placed in the cell with me a few days later. I knew her from the compound, but never really made a connection with her. She was much younger and facing many years. From what I heard, she was doing her time the hard way, making trouble for herself on a regular basis. I spent several days and night talking to her, praying over her, and even filing motions on her behalf. I knew very little about filing motions, but I was willing to help in hopes that she gets a sentence reduction. On June 19th, it was late in the evening, I was on the bottom bunk reading my Bible, and my cell mate was on the top bunk reading a hood novel. I noticed a bloody hand holding a small shaving razor extended from the top bunk... I jumped up terrified! "Here Bunkie, take this from me!" A soft weakened voice said franticly. Quickly, I gathered my thoughts, grabbed her towel from the rustic bedrail, and wrapped it around her arm. The blood didn't stop!

I jumped down and began kicking, banging on the door for a guard to come. "Lord please don't let her faint on me!" I climbed in bed with her, throwing my body across her arm to apply pressure. The entire time, I was praying over her as well. Her eyes began to roll back, and I screamed louder for the guards. The two young female guards that were on duty stood at the metal door looking through the glass while I did the job of medical. They had the nerve to tell me that they were not coming into the cell until medical came because they were not going to come in contact with her bodily fluids. I went from praying to cursing them out! Look how the devil works! Here it is, I was being very selfless trying to help her, not knowing her medical history. In such a situation, it didn't even matter! The darn guards wouldn't even help her! "Heavenly father, thank you for standing in the midst!" I silently prayed.

When Medical came in, they drug her to medical and tore our cell up looking for the cutting tool. I was taken to the shower area and fainted, having never experienced anything like that in my life! I think that was the drawing point for me! I had experienced all I could take! I was tired and ready to go home! I was missing my kids so much.

Later I was able to make a 15 minute phone call. I called my mom and just so happen, my little angel was in the office with her. Chyna got on the phone and I began to explain why they haven't heard from me. She stopped me and said, "It's ok momma, you just have to learn discipline like you always tell us!"

A stream of tears came down my checks, and my heart melted even more! Once again my children were giving me the encouragement I needed to go on.

Chapter 16

Time was winding down. On June 30th, God gave me a revelation assuring me that I was going home and that D.H.O. would not take any of my good days. In that dream, he allowed me to see some things that would assure me of his promise!

Mr. Hughes, the same counselor that came to escort me into the prison when I turned myself in, was the same man God used to assure me that I was leaving on my promised date. I had a dream of the exact attire Mr. Hughes would be wearing on the day of my hearing and a conversation he and I would have when he stopped by my cell after the hearing.

On July 5th, early that morning, I was told to get dressed to see D.H.O. As the guard walked me around to the room, my attention was drawn to Mr. Hughes standing to my right, wearing a white button up shirt, black tie, and black slacks. I became nervous because in my dream he was wearing a red tie. I began to pray silently because I could feel my faith trying to slip through the cracks of those raggedly tan shower slides I had on. When the representative began to question me about the incident, she told me that I had the right to request a staff member to be present on my behalf. "Can you call Chaplin Anderson to sit in on my behalf?" She looked at me funny, I guess no one ever asked for a preacher to represent them. Difference was, I knew to ask for the person that knew my character best!

Sure enough, he came and assured me that everything would be just fine! While we waited for the hearing to start, he and I made small talk. As usual, he asked me, "So, what have you been feeding your mind?" I explained about all the scriptures I had read, books, meditations, and business plans that I had wrote during the 3 weeks I had been in the S.H.U. As the meeting started, the lady had a very nasty attitude and was complaining about having to come over to the building in the rain. I side-eyed the Chaplin with worry in my eyes and he signaled for me to let him handled it. When it was time for her to make a decision, she looked at me and said, "You better be lucky! You been doing some praying to somebody because Regional already processed you out of the system for you to go home. I was about to order you to serve 45 more days in prison!"

"YES! THANK YOU JESUS!" I shouted like I had just won the lottery. I tried to keep my composure as I sat there in handcuffs. The Chaplin stood up, smiling with his chest poked out, cocky and confident, because he was sure of our Father's Grace and Mercy! "You may return back to your cell until they call you to pack up!" I was told.

My heart was dancing for joy. I walked out the door and Mr. Hughes was still standing in the same spot, this time to my left. "Mr. Hughes, what happened to the red tie you were supposed to put on this morning?" I asked the question with a smile on my face, causing a sign of confusion to fall upon his face. I was back in my cell all of maybe 10 minutes when Mr. Hughes came to the door and peeped in through the glass. I jumped up and grabbed a set of paper that was at the foot of the bed. I was expecting him, because God had already prepared me for this visit by way of my dream.

"How did you know I was going to wear a red tie? I took it off because I couldn't find my socks to match it," he told me. I slid the paper under the door that I had been using to record my dreams on because I couldn't have my journal in the cell with me. I asked him to read the dream dated for June 30th. His mouth dropped, full of surprise. I told him, "Not every person that comes into a prison is there because they deserve to be! Some of us are just passing through on a God-given assignment."

It was at that very moment that it all made sense to me. Just as God told the Israelites, while in captivity, you will be trained to do the work He has called you to do! I cried out to God, praising and thanking Him! First for allowing me to go home to my babies on the date that I promised them, but secondly, for using me in a mighty way to help and be a blessing unto others. I made a vow to God in that very moment to follow His lead and do the work I was called to do!

I'm not sure where Mr. Hughes is today, but I'm sure he's a changed man and certainly a BELIEVER! He went and told a few of his colleagues what happened and Ms. Gainer came and asked me if I could tell her the lottery number! (LOL) It's not that easy, though. If so, I would be rich myself! What I do know is, there's a great reward for an obedient servant of God! There was just one more thing I had to do before I left.

I wrote a letter to D.H.O. on behalf of the lady that I fought. I asked them to please dismiss any charge that she might be facing because I felt it was only right being hat I was going home and she was still facing roughly 16 years. I'm not sure if they let her go back to the compound right away, but God assured me that He would work in her favor!

Chapter 17

The morning had finally come for my FREEDOM WALK!

July 8th, 2016 around 10:30 a.m. I was called: "Harris pack up!" Sounded like the Lord was calling me home! My sister Chat was scheduled to pick me up. I got dressed into the Victoria Secret tights and tank my god-sister had mailed in and left everything else I owned except my Bible, pictures, business plans, and dream book!

As I walked out, I spotted my sister Chat waving me into her direction. I was so excited to be free, I didn't care that my hair was nappy while she recorded me. "Surprise!" Chyna and Daylon jumped out from behind a parked truck, scaring the life out of me! I was so happy to see them! "Who are you people? Where did my babies go?" They had gotten so tall. Just in that little span of time, seemed like I missed a lifetime of maturity!

We hugged and hurried to the truck. I didn't want to spend another second on that property! I went to Atlanta for the weekend before reporting to Mississippi Federal Probation Office.

Coming home was very refreshing, but believe it or not, I missed out on a lot in 13 months.

Technology changes daily and my kids were tremendously advanced. I was so proud to see and hear about all of their many accomplishments. Life was going by so fast as I tried to piece things back together and make a way to provide for my children and me.

There were several close friends and family members that made sure my children had the things they needed while I was away. Those same people extended their gratitude towards me when I came home. I thank all of them, and want them to know they have not been forgotten by me.

I went back to Mississippi and stayed at my mother's house for a few months while I got myself together. I began doing hair the same week I was released, right from my mother's sunroom again. I reached out to my old clients to let them know I was home and back to work. Most of them returned while others had ventured off to other stylists. Business picked back up really fast. Within two weeks, I began looking for a salon. I reached out to several people I knew in the hair industry and searched Craig's List for something in my price range... No luck! I began to grow very frustrated until God placed me on the heart of an old friend that I'd met and done business with previously, Jas! Jas owned a salon in Jackson, but lived in Georgia. She reached out and told me she had some bundles of hair for me, but God had a better plan. Jas branded some of the best flatirons on the market and they were one of my favorite tools. One day, while doing a silk press, my flatiron went out. I called her up: "Hey Jas, it's B! Please tell me someone is at your salon? I need to purchase some new flatirons ASAP!"

"Hey B," She said to me, "I'm in town now, you can meet me at the salon." When I arrived, Jas was sitting, taking a break waiting on her next client. She and I began talking and God simultaneously answered both of our prayers! I was looking for a salon to conduct business and Jas was looking for someone to run her salon while she's away in Georgia conducting business. DIVINE APPOINTMENT!

It's all in God's timing! She and I began cleaning up and rearranging the shop. We even went and had keys made! While we were riding, I told Jas about a really close friend of mine that does hair as well, Shanti. I wanted her to be my business partner. When Jas told me the amount she wanted for rent, I knew it was nobody but God making a way once again! You see, there's power in unity and only a God-fearing human would know that! I called Shanti, extended the offer, we set a meet and greet for that evening, and made a toast to partnership and wealth!

Business picked up tremendously! I was told, the best place you can put a person is in a position to make money! God don't judge us by our hands, He judges us by our hearts!

Now that I had a steady flow of income, I still felt a sense of emptiness. I was attending my childhood church which I had been a member of since I was a young child, but I wasn't getting that "Fullness" I had experienced in Tallahassee. Dr. Anderson had opened my eyes through his teaching in such a way that made it uncomfortable to sit under the teaching of anything less powerful. That spiritual connection is a must! I had to find another church home, and I knew just the place: Jackson Revival Center!

From the very moment of driving onto the parking lot of their new location near Byram, MS, I felt that welcoming spirit that I had been missing! I knew that I was sure to receive a full course meal every time I walked into the building! My cousin Tosha and I would meet there and worship together. Pastor Biard has the most nurturing and anointing spirit! I promise you, I would wake up late forgetting to eat breakfast, but after leaving church I would be full and sleepy! Like a baby, I think the sermons were whipping me like a terrible two year old! I'm so thankful for her. My son was highly active in the youth ministry at our previous church so I didn't force him to leave, but Chyna and I joined Jackson Revival Center. For once in my life, I felt as if everything had finally come together and flowing in the path God needed me to be in.

Chapter 18

While I was away, I made God a promise that I was done having sex until He sent my husband. (Side Eye) Guess I shouldn't have made that promise out loud, because the enemy knows our weakness even when we don't!

Late one Saturday evening, Mid-October 2016 (It was the weekend of Jackson State homecoming), Clarion, my cousin/sister, Shanti, and I were walking onto the stadium parking lot to go tailgating. "Whoa ladies! Y'all not gonna show a brother no love?!" It was the voice of a very familiar actor/rapper in the industry. Clarion and Shanti became tickled and engaged in conversation with him while my attention was drawn to the guy standing to the right of him. He was a very well groomed, nicely tailored man with salt and pepper hair and a physique of an athlete. The kind of man that stood back while his friend took Snapchat pictures with my friends. "Y'all just ignored him," I said, extending my hand. "Hi, I'm Bianca." He gave me one of the most attractive side smirks and said, "It's ok baby, they can get the pictures, I'm gone get the check! I like you already, follow me on IG!" He took my phone and entered his Instagram name into my search engine and followed himself from my page, his business and personal page. I guess that was an informal way of him telling me to check his credentials. We exchanged numbers, they told us where they would be partying at for the night, and we parted ways.

The next morning as I was walking to the car leaving church, my phone vibrated from the bottom of my purse. A New York number displayed across the screen and a charming accent came through the car speaker when I answered the call. My face lit up with this pink glow, it was "Mr. I'm gone get the check" from the night before. We talked and exchanged laughter as I opened the sunroof and played "The Truth" by India Arie on iTunes. He asked if he could see me, and if my cousin and I would like to join them for lunch. "We want to go somewhere that has the best fried chicken and macaroni and cheese," he said. I laughed and told him, "That would be my kitchen!" I declined his offer to go out to a restaurant, but instead, offered to cook at the house and play card games. Jackson is very small and I felt the need to keep this one private, at least in that moment.

That evening was so refreshing, and our chemistry instantly connected as we got to know each other. He told me that he was currently living in Atlanta and offered me to come visit. After a few weeks of talking on the phone and FaceTime, I accepted the invitation and traveled to Atlanta to visit. This man touched me in ways I had never experienced! Everything about him was different than the men I used to date. He was older, well educated, and arrogant in a sense. The energy was weird. The same things that pushed me away from other men, somehow pulled me closer to him. I felt challenged when I was in his presence and that had never happened to me before.

I began to crave everything about this man! I can remember my grandmother coming to me in a dream saying that she didn't trust the man with grey hair. I brushed it off and certainly knew she wasn't referring to him. I introduced him to my family and close friends, explaining "It's something about him, I just don't know what it is!" Life lessons had taught me to pay close attention to my intuition. We exchanged visits when our schedules permitted, getting to know each other on a very intimate level, but the relationship was stagnant.

While lying in the bed of a Downtown Jackson hotel, I began to feel convicted. I woke "Mr." up. "Babe, can we talk," I asked. He rolled over, extending his arm, motioning for me to lay my head on his chest. I began the conversation by sharing my feelings and insight on a spiritual level. I knew that would be a sensitive conversation, especially since I was playing on the devil's playground.

 We talked for hours, going back and forth about our different views. He was more of an astrologist, while my faith was centered around Jesus Christ. "Lord, he knows how to capture me every time!" Everything about our relationship felt so good to my flesh, but I knew it was detrimental for my soul!

Time was flying as I kept busy, working long hours in the salon, being a full-time mother, attending school functions and all of Daylon's athletic games, and maintaining my sanity in my personal life.

Dear Mom,

I just want to tell you thank you for all the hard work and your patience with me. You have worked hard to buy me what I wanted. You are always telling me that I do not need this or that, but you buy it anyways. You have been there for me every time I have needed you. I love you and I know I do not do what I suppose to some times, but I work hard in school to make you happy.

I Love You Mom,

Daylon

I had saved up a nice piece of change and wanted to expand in business, build a brand, and more services for our clients. I consulted with Jas and Shanti, letting them know what I was looking to do. We agreed to work towards expanding together, but I didn't see actions being taken so I branched off to do my own thing. There's one thing I do know, God can only bless you as far as you are willing to grow!

My search was becoming a headache! I wanted a certain building structure so that each new service would have it's own private area. I remember sitting in church, crying, feeling like everything was coming together and falling apart at the same time. I was praying asking God to do things I wanted Him to bless me with, forgetting about the things I promised Him I would or wouldn't do! Because He is a FAITHFUL GOD, even when we fall short of His glory, we are still blessed with the desires of our heart. Things were lining up, but I was uncomfortable receiving them because of my wrongdoings.

Pastor Biard was preaching this particular Sunday. She stated that all hell was about to break loose in your life and heaven is going to open up at the same time! I started screaming, crying, and jumping. I remember feeling like I wanted to rip my skin off! Guilt was riding me like a bull! It was in that very moment of that sermon that I realized that making God promises and not keeping them only hurts you mentally! From that point on, I learned to just pray for strength to endure while I grow strong enough to overcome certain situations. During that same sermon, she said, "You are going to walk into a building this week and when you see it, you are going to say I'LL TAKE THAT!" She even mentioned that it's going to be structured just like you have dreamed about. I began to praise God louder because I felt like that prophesy was for me! Needless to say, that same week, on a Tuesday, I went to view several buildings and the very last one was exactly what I wanted! "Lord thank you for allowing me to receive that prophesy as a blessing!" I signed the lease and paid my brother Earl to start renovating right away.

Chapter 19

Within six months of being released from prison, coming home without a dime to my name, God blessed me with my own home, salon, and a new car!

Meanwhile, all the plans and promises that I made Him were put on the back burner! Selfishly, I was just living life… existing! My kids were so happy and through the eyes of everyone else, I appeared to be extremely happy as well! I guess that glow that God blessed me with was shining brighter than the hell I was experiencing on the inside.

Although I had accomplished a lot, I felt as though I had not accomplished enough! My five sisters and I are very close. We don't always see eye to eye, but we love each other unconditionally!

We formed a group text which suddenly became an outlet for us to vent amongst each other, motivate, and discipline each other as well. Those chats motivated me in my weakest points! They always say I'm the mean or tough one, but truth is even I grow weary! We feed off each other's strength which pushed me to continue striving for the stars. Not only do I want success for my children and I, but for my siblings as well! I used to write letters and emails to my oldest sister telling her we should form a non-profit or ministry. Amongst the seven of us, Earl included, had been through enough hell to heal a nation from our experiences alone!

March 3rd, 2017 I opened my new salon! It was so beautiful! It was my baby! I prayed and planned for it. I was so excited. My kids and I prayed over it then named her Chos3n Beauty Bar! While in captivity, the Holy Spirit placed the brand name Chosen in my heart. I began to write and make plans for every entity that I wanted under this brand on a tablet and dated it. Then I thought, there's a story behind this. Let me add the 3 and make it Chos3n! That way, when people see it, they will ask me to explain the name and in turn I could briefly testify! -Proverbs 16:3

To see those things begin to form and manifest has been a blessing within itself. I extended the olive branch to others and gave them space within the salon at a very low rate. I prayed and asked God to send me a team that was willing to work together, grow, but most importantly, pray together! Business was flourishing! I was so proud of myself. "Mr." even came in town and sat in the salon for hours, greeting and interacting with the clients as they received various services.

We sponsored several charity events privately, allowing God get the glory, and ran specials on a regular basis to give back to the community. God has been a blessing to all of us, so it was only right to do so!

Early one warm sunny morning in May 2017 I received a text message while getting dressed for work. I dropped everything and immediately dialed the number attached to the text. It was my friend Tameika telling me to check on Keshia, something terrible had happened! I called Keshia's phone, on the second ring, her friend answered. "Keshia is ok," the friend said. "It's Sky."

My knees buckled and my soul left my body! I grabbed my purse, hair all over my head, crying and praying to the most high God all the way down highway 18 that my niece was alright! I knew this had to be just a huge mistake and a big confusion. When I pulled up to Keshia's house and seen my sister rocking in that chair, I knew that nobody but God would be able to see her through this!

The pain that I felt then and the emptiness I feel now was like losing one of my children. I remembered the incident with my Bunkie and instantly dropped to Keshia's feet and began praying for my sister as I wept in her lap. I asked God to find my deepest inner strength and allow me to intercede for my sister! She had been through so much.

I closely watched her level of strength as she fought and beat breast cancer. She made me stronger without even knowing I was weak! Now, it was time for me to return that strength because my sister was going to need it!

Keshia and I are not blood sisters, but with the spiritual bond we have blood couldn't make us any closer. As we prepared for Skyla's home-going, friends and family gathered daily to keep Keshia and her two son's spirits lifted. While leaving the burial, I received a text from my mother wanting to know where I was. I picked up the phone to call her because my gut told me that a text was not the right option for the response I was about to get. "Ma, what's wrong?" I heard the tears and pain through her voice when she answered the phone. "Bianca, get here! Uncle Alvin is gone!" I came to a complete stop in the left southbound lane on I-55 as traffic was zooming around me. All I could do was scream and pound my fist on the steering wheel. "Lord help ME!" I couldn't take another heartache, tragedy, or ounce of bad news! I had taken all I could take!

I was told that death come in 3s but that pain was enough to last a lifetime! I was renting Uncle Alvin's house for months after coming home from prison. He had been my favorite uncle since I was a little girl. Whenever I needed him, whether I was right or wrong, he was there with no questions asked. I had gotten so used to him coming by the house to pick up his mail and to see what I cooked. All sorts of buried pain and sorrow resurfaced, smothering me like a pillow, covering my face in a taped-up cardboard box!

I woke up with this feeling for roughly three or four weeks. I didn't even want to go in to the salon to work. I called my best friend Shameka and asked her to pray with me. She agreed without questions or judgement and told me she would be over after work. Shameka kept her word and came right away. She and I went over to the salon to pray over it first. After praying and asking God to remove all tainted spirits and break all chains of bondage, we set out to my house. Along the ride back, she looked me square in the face and told me, "Beedie, it's someone around you that you have to let go! God placed this on my heart, but I had to wait for the right time to share this with you so you would be receptive." I looked at her with a puzzling face and said, "Who? I don't hang with anybody for real…" She explained that God didn't show her a face but this person is a female and I trust them with my business and secrets. She even said there will be signs and I will ignore them, but in order to get to the next level where God is calling you to you have to let her go!

I sat there looking puzzled as we pulled into my driveway. We prayed over my house and said our sisterly goodbyes. I was home alone, candles burning, and gospel music playing loud through my portable speaker. I fell down on my knees and cried out to God asking Him to lead me, redirect me, cover me, but most of all, remove EVERYBODY that was standing in the way of my blessings.

Chapter 20

The later part of June, 2017 I woke up and said, "I want out!" Out of my misery, out of pain, bondage, and anything else that reminded me of everything I had gone through! "We are leaving Mississippi!"

I discussed my decision with my children and Jessie. Jessie and I had always had a very close bond since I was 16 years old. Even when we disagreed on things, I valued his opinion because he has always had my best interest at heart. Jessie has been away in federal prison for almost a decade, but we keep a close knit bond. He has the heart of a giant and a genuine love for my children and me.

"I think you should go," he told me. "If moving is going to be the outlet to a better life for you and those kids, that's your move!" I took that as confirmation because normally, if he had a bad vibe about something, he would say it and stand firm on it! I was on federal probation so again, I had to reach out to my probation officer and ask if I could get a traveling pass to Georgia. I explained the things that I was going through that influenced my decision to move. Not all officers of authority are compassionate, but I was blessed to cross paths with those of great morals and character.

I was awarded the opportunity to travel and look for a house while I align things for my children such as school. I kept God at the center of everything and trusted that He would go before me and pave the way. It only took me a few days to find a house, and I went back to Mississippi to get my kids and furniture. As I was riding back, I began to worry about what I would do with my salon, but then it hit me. A few weeks prior, and old friend from hair school stopped by inquiring about a salon suite. I called Byrd and offered her to sub-lease my fully furnished salon, and she agreed to take it! I packed and planned quietly, because I didn't want anyone to discourage me, not even my family. Traveling back and forth for a month straight, I finally had everything in order.

Now my money had gotten low, but giving up was not an option. I reached out to my God-brother, Renzo. Our families had been close since I was in grade school. "Brother I need you..." and there was no questions asked! He was going through a rough situation of his own, but as always, he put himself on the backburner and made sure I was ok. Giving me his last, I assured him that I would always make sure he's ok. I'm a woman of my word! Every obstacle that could hit me, happened, trying to block me from leaving! I promised myself that if I had to live in my car, I was leaving Jackson! It wasn't so much as to pain that was driving me away, but purpose inspiring me to leave! I knew God had a calling over my life. When we do everything we want, omitting what He wants, God has a way of making us very uncomfortable!

July, 2017 my mother and I spent hours in the rain directing the traffic of the U-haul being loaded with the help of my nephews. Once that house was clear and clean, I-20 East became the highway to heaven! Chyna and Daylon were already awaiting us at my sister Chat's house in Georgia. It was late when we arrived, but we picked the kids up and made pallets on the floor until the next morning. It was something about the aura of this house… very peaceful and spacious. I would spend hours meditating while we decorate, allowing my mind to roam freely. I set up an area in our home to service clients, but I was more driven to the area in my bedroom designed for a home office. I could slowly feel myself drifting away from the desire to do hair or even be around people period.

I learned something very valuable in that Silent Season. I learned that I shouldn't be trying to build something when I was supposed to be cultivating my spirit. I was supposed to use that season to spend time with God, grow, and rest in Him – not step out on faith and try to do something out of His timing. How many of us are making "faith moves" when we are supposed to be resting. You will find yourself tired because you built something that wasn't even for you. Heather Lindsey - "Silent Seasons"

I began to build this wall, blocking others out and caging myself in! My tolerance was very thin, my desire for "Mr." was even fading away!

I thought that being in Georgia would enhance our relationship, but the ugly truth finally surfaced… He was married! He lied and still denies it to this day! He told me the wedding pictures that I had seen were clips from a reality show that has yet to air! Now, the old me would have spazzed out and made his life a living hell, but when you pray and ask God to reveal things, He don't sugar coat or exclude your favorites! That lie was the best thing he could have done for me. I walked away and wished him well! "Thank you Father!"

After a while, Jessie was the only person I desired to talk to. He's just so genuine. Yes he wrecks my nerves, but he's genuine! We began to shift gears, motivating one another to be better people, even exchanging business ideas and encouraging ourselves to touch a different realm in life. Anyone can do wrong by you, but try doing right! After years of allowing disappointment to control me, I mastered it! I now control my peace! A few years ago, I was listening to the gospel station here in Atlanta and the lady said, "He who angers you, controls you!" Once you grasp the concept of that, I promise you better days will began to form in that very moment!

Mid November 2017 my kids had left to go to Mississippi with my sister. I made plans to stay home and complete all the work that was behind, including this book. Once they were safely on the road, I silenced my phone and began writing. While writing, the Holy Spirit spoke to me so loud and clear! "Clean your house!" I started looking around, puzzled because I kept a clean house. "Lord, you can't be serious right now?" I wanted to work while there were no distractions. I ignored it and continued to write. "Clean this house, from the inside out!" This time, the words came from

Pandora playing through the speakers on my phone by Isaac Carree and R. Kelly. I was a complete wreck on the inside! I was crying so hard, my tears began to soak the paper I was writing on.

I stood up to go blow my nose and fell down, too weak to even walk. God wanted me to kneel, so He put me there! I began to feel so hot that I took off all my clothes and crawled to my bathroom. As I reached for the sink, my attention was drawn to my closet. I left the water running and crawled into the closet. Closing the door, I cried out to God, "Here I am, naked, exposed, cleanse me oh God! Make me whole again..." I began to make some promises that I knew I wouldn't go back on my word with and attached deadlines to them this time! As I was praying for others, I could hear Jessie saying, "You got to give God some things and stick to them!" I told God that if He help me cleanse my house and restore me 100-fold, I would do all the work he required of me 100%.

I asked Him to remove me from toxic situations and remove toxic people from my space! They tell me that the tongue is powerful... I dare you to use your innately given power and ask God to move on your behalf in a positive aspect! I can promise you, He's going to move, and He's going to REMOVE everybody that he feel should be replaced!

Now, I have to be perfectly honest: I tried to bargain with God because some people I wanted to keep around and certain things I wasn't ready to give up! This was especially true when it came to pleasing my flesh! There's this one guy I've known since I was young. We have been in each other's company for years because we have mutual friends. When things went left field with Mr, "T" and I would confide in each other because things in his relationship were rocky as well.

Dinner and drinks turned into lustful romance! T would literally drive my soul to hell and back! He knew just how to please my body physically! He was that "friend" that you can trust everything with, but my soul was paying the price for that "good time!" God said, "NO! He must go too!" It was a struggle, but I know the reward for my obedience would be much greater! I've struggled, even came close to losing my house, BUT GOD said, "I know the plans I have for you, declares the Lord! Plans to prosper you and not to harm you, plans to give you hope and a future. Then you will call on me and come and pray to me, and I will listen to you. You will seek me and find me when you seek me with all your heart. I will be found by you, declares the Lord, and will bring you back from captivity. I will gather you from all the nations and places where I have banished you, declares the Lord, and will bring you back to the place from which I carried you into exile!" -Jeremiah 29:11-14

So here I am, a legal resident of Georgia! Transformed, ready and prepared to do the great work of my Father! Trust me, it won't be easy, but it's surely going to be worth it! Yes, I may have made a few mistakes, and they too were worth it!

Destiny, Eugenia, and Candace are now home! God turned Candace's 12 year federal sentence into a 7 year bid and declared favor over her life! Candace and I have expanded our sisterhood by joining forces in partnership to be advocates of God's glory and help millions of people obtain wealth byway of our God given talents. As we work towards building an empire from the stones that were meant to tear us down, we will be awaiting thousands of our fellow sisters to return home and share their story! "The best is yet to come!"

What "A High Cost to Low Living" means to you

So now I truly understand that the life I was living had been ordained by God!

My Creator needed me to go through a series of trials so that I would be an experienced living witness to His children!

We all have gone through the same hell, just different devils! You have read my definition and how it fits my life. I reached out to 5 women of different races and backgrounds to see what this quote meant to them.

Surprisingly, we all met as strangers but shared similar pain. After reading their definitions and how it applied to their life, I invite you to share your journey with us!

One thing for certain: the high cost of living these days is nothing in comparison to the cost of living high. Thorough out my life I have seen drugs claim so much goodness, especially from the innocent. After all, they are the ones who suffer the most.

Within less than a year of using and selling amphetamines, I lost my business, my home and my husband who died at only 36 while in state prison. In addition to that I was sentenced to 240 months in prison! My children have been forced to limit their relationship with their mother to visitation rooms and 15 min phone calls.

I can only pray, at some point, someone will extend a hand to help those of us who suffer from/with addiction, whether it be a passion we have for drugs or money. Help us so we may return to our role as mom or dad, brother or sister, son or daughter. Why? Because many of us still have the heart, the will to be that.

Granted, when we hit bottom, we lowered everything from our dreams to our inhibitions. But in that very place where we, "the lesser" live, you will find some very loving and inspirational people. Ones who fall harder and love deeper than any other.

Sonya Pittman

43 years old

Caucasian

How to start this topic?

First and foremost, Being that I've been in and out the federal system since I was 18 years old, I've become a prisoner for the decisions I've made in life. I've become a prisoner to loneliness and hurt because of those decisions.

Losing my mother at 15 years old left me to fend for myself and led me to make the decisions I've made in life, not really seeing or realizing the person I was really hurting was my beautiful daughter.

Too many times all I needed was someone to pull me through. Being so blind that God was the only way. Not really having help while incarcerated I learned to humble myself and be grateful for the little things in life, but having to go through this was the worse.

Being used to getting things on my own and coming to this and being too prideful to even ask for help was something that was really hard. Living the life that I did because I felt

I had no choice led me to this high cost of hurt, pain and loneliness. Not only for myself but for my beautiful angel.

It took coming in and out to actually see that our Father is the only person that can help me in this life. Coming from nothing but a small locker with hardly anything inside, losing faith and losing hope was the high cost. Finding God is the only way to pay that cost. I've sold drugs since I was 15 years old because I couldn't get a job since I was too young.

By the time I was 18 years old all I had was all taken away. I've been in and out the system since then. All that made me empty inside and selfish.

I went from having it all—well thinking I had it all—to having nothing at all.

What was the only thing that was keeping me going you ask? That was the love of my beautiful daughter, and the love and strength

of women I barely know as well as the love of
God.

Destiny Neira

26 years old

Hispanic

High cost to low living can mean giving up something of great value to satisfy a "need": ex. Your self-worth, values, your kids, etc.

Low living is being in a life without meaning. You may look one way on the outside, but emotionally you're depleted. You may have it going on to everyone else, but behind closed doors you're lost, living a lie.

But now looking at this theme "High Cost to Low Living" to me reminds me of how God rendered His One and only Son (high costs) for our sins (low living). Jesus, being King of Kings, humbled himself down, never exalting himself or puffing himself up. He never treated us like we treated him! Instead he loves us and forgives us, regardless of who we are, because he knows whose we are.

He being King of Kings, Lord of Lords, obeyed our Father's command, living like a peasant, being mistreated until death.

There is a high cost to love living. We have to set ourselves low before others, and the Lord will exalt us on high. All we have to do is express humility, compassion, forgiveness, patience, grace, mercy and loving kindness towards all.

One of my favorite scriptures is Hebrews 13:1-2 which reminds us "Let brotherly love continue. Do not neglect to show hospitality to strangers for thereby some have entertained angels unawares."

We have to keep that in mind as we give up pride (high cost) for a life of humility and love (low living).

Eugenia Williams

46

Black/Hispanic

To me the statement "There is a high cost to low living" means many things:

- First it reminds me of two sayings that I grew up hearing: "Penny wise, pound foolish" (which originated in the British culture where there money currency consist of pennies and pounds). The interpretation is that those who buy cheap things that cost only pennies will end up spending more pounds, because the penny items do not last long, and one has to keep on spending pennies which in the end amount to a high cost! The second saying that I was reminded of is "Cheap buying is expensive buying." The interpretation here is the same as the one expressed in pennies and pounds, and that is buying cheap things that are not durable lead to one having to replace the item many times over, which in the end leads to a high cost for that item.

- Secondly when I read the statement that there is a 'high cost to low living' I also thought about the literal meaning of that statement, that in life it never pays to cut corners or attempting to get over because in the end one gets caught in one's own web.

- Third, the statement struct me at a personal level. The reason? It reminds me that I should strive at all times to live up to my full God-given potential. Here I have to state that in all human beings there is a bright or good side, as well as a dark side with negative tendencies. At any given time a person goes between these two opposing poles, and that to me is what life is about. Perfection in human beings to me will forever be a noble goal to strive towards, but it is almost impossible to achieve, even for believing Christians with faith.

- Finally the statement tells me that I should be mindful of consequences that come from my actions, because negative actions lead to dangerous and heavy penalties.

Mickal Kamuvaka

68 years old

Afrian descent

"There is a high cost to low living."

When Bianca first gave me this assignment I grimaced at it.

My first thought was if only I knew then what I know now I would have made better choices in life. I would have never ever put myself in a position to be separated from my babies.

All I was trying to do was give them the things my mother and grandmother only dreamed about giving us. Now after looking at and reading this slogan and pondering on it, I can now say Father God, I thank you for your grace and mercy. This high cost to this low living, you protected me in the midst of my mess. The mess that I caused for myself, the devastation that I have caused my children.

I blamed everybody for this mess that I caused including the Prosecutor and the Judge. As I'm writing this I have to laugh to myself, because even through the high cost that man wanted me to pay for this low living my

God still loved me so much that he said "12 ½ years, 151 months... Not so!"

Won't he do it?

It's not just about the poor choices I made: leaving my children, losing my worldly possessions temporarily... The lesson in this that I have learned is only—and I do mean only—what you do for Christ will last. The impact that this experience has had on me is something I won't forget. I will one day be in a position to share it not only with my children but others who are willing to listen.

Put God first and all things will be added. Bianca, I think you for choosing me to be a part of this assignment.

Candace N. Wilson

45

Black

What "A High Cost to Low Living" Means to Me

_____

_____

_____

_____

_____

_____

_____

_____

_____

_____

_____

_____

_____

_____

_____

Bianca is available for speaking engagements, book-signings and conferences.

Contact her using the information below:

Bianca Harris

601-874-5723

chos3nconsultants@gmail.com

Instagram: chos3n_iam

Facebook: Cho3n Beauty Bar